365 Quote Quest: Reflecting on Vital Quotations

by Paul H. Cornies

I0425051

Foreward

The unexamined life is not worth living. ~ Socrates

The premise of this book is to offer some of the wisdom of classical and modern authors and to encourage reflection on their perspectives. These meditations are an outgrowth of 365 Quote Quest, an ongoing daily blog. As well, my other blog Quoteflections expands upon this premise and gleans information from current events and opinion.

I am a retired educator living in southwestern Ontario, Canada. I received a Master's of History from the University of Waterloo in 1974 with a focus in intellectual history. I taught English in high school for 32 years and served as a literacy coach and coordinator.

In the classroom I often had a quote for the day and we would discuss its meaning and sometimes write a journal. Several guiding questions helped students to come to an understanding of the quote and of themselves.

I hope you enjoy the quotes and may the reflective questions help to enrich your daily life.

Paul Cornies

Table of Contents:

Chapter 1: January Quotations – Page 2
Chapter 2: February – Page 12
Chapter 3: March – Page 21
Chapter 4: April – Page 30
Chapter 5: May – Page 40
Chapter 6: June – Page 49
Chapter 7: July – Page 59
Chapter 8: August – Page 68
Chapter 9: September – Page 77
Chapter 10: October – Page 86
Chapter 11: November – Page 94
Chapter 12: December – Page 103

Chapter 1: January Quotations

#1 How we Spend our Days

How we spend our days is, of course, how we spend our lives.
~Annie Dillard

-What generalizations can you make about your daily activities, attitudes, interests, and lifestyle?
- How happy are you happy with your daily regimen?
-What small steps can you make to begin to transform or enrich your days?

#2 Happiness and Serving

I don't know what your destiny will be, but one thing I know: the only ones among you who will be really happy are those who will have sought and found how to serve. ~ Albert Schweitzer

- How does this quote seem to counter the dominant societal perspectives today?
- How actively do you seek out opportunities to serve?
- When have you found happiness in serving?
- What steps can you take to enrich your service opportunities?

#3 Careless and Tidy

Be careless in your dress if you must, but keep a tidy soul.
~Mark Twain

-To what extent are your decisions made out of self interest and vanity?
-How important are appearance and status in your daily life?
-What does Twain mean by a tidy soul?
-What are enduring values?

#4 Appreciate the Climb

Live your life each day as you would climb a mountain. An occasional glance toward the summit keeps the goal in mind, but many beautiful scenes are to be observed from each new vantage point. Climb slowly, steadily, enjoying each passing moment; and the view from the summit will serve as a fitting climax for the journey. ~ Harold B. Melchart

-What can you appreciate about Melchart's analogy?
-To what extent might your daily pursuit of goals detract you from the beauty all around?
-How can you bring more joy into your daily life?

#5 Food Conundrum

Vegetables are a must on a diet. I suggest carrot cake, zucchini bread, and pumpkin pie. ~Jim Davis

The local groceries are all out of broccoli, Loccoli. ~ Roy Blount Jr.

-Why do many gravitate to the 'junk' foods?
-How would you describe your diet and nutritional value of what you eat?
-What steps can you take to enrich your diet?

#6 Challenges of Child Raising

Your children need your presence more than your presents. ~ Jesse Jackson

-Everybody loves presents. What are good presents for children, the questionable ones?
-For parents what does 'presence' mean while raising children? Provide specific examples.
-Why is this quote particularly relevant in today's world?

#7 The Tissue of Every Day Life

Life, we learn too late, is in the living, in the tissue of every day and hour. ~ Stephen Leacock

-Why is there a tone of regret in the quotation?
-This tissue of life includes what dimensions?
-What opportunities have you neglected, or captured recently?

#8 Enthusiasm over Wisdom

I prefer the errors of enthusiasm to the indifference of wisdom. ~ Anatole France

-Where have you seen the lifeblood of enthusiasm?

-When and why is human error a good thing?
-Why do we need to temper our wisdom?

#9 Tis a Gift to be Simple

'Tis the gift to be simple,
'tis the gift to be free,
'Tis the gift to come down where we ought to be,
And when we find ourselves in the place just right,
Twill be in the valley of love and delight.
When true simplicity is gain'd,
To bow and to bend we shan't be asham'd,
To turn, turn will be our delight, Till by turning, turning we
come round right.

~ 1848, Shaker song by Joseph Brackett

- Why is it difficult to live simply and humbly?
- How does simplicity and humility foster freedom and happiness?
- When have you felt release as the song describes so well?

#10 No Duty is More Urgent

No duty is more urgent than that of returning thanks. ~James Allen

-How often do you take for granted that others know how grateful you are of them?
-What can you do this week to show gratitude to the caring people around you?
-What overtures of thanks can you make to the peripheral people in your life?

#11 The only Gift

The only gift is a portion of thyself. ~ Ralph Waldo Emerson

- Why is a purchased gift often the more desirable option?
- What gift of a person's time and talents have you appreciated?
- What personal gift can you provide to a person this week?

#12 Hear, See, Do

I hear and I forget. I see and I remember. I do and I understand.
~ Chinese proverb

- Think of a presenter/teacher who really helped you to learn by doing.
- How can presenters/teachers more thoroughly engage their audiences?
- When have you taught yourself and/or someone a skill?

#13 Moving on from Mistakes

There is no mistake so great as the mistake of not going on. ~ William Blake (1757-1827, poet, painter)

- Blake, repeats 'mistake', for emphasis. Why?
- What do people often do after making a mistake?
- How should one move on after making a mistake?

#14 Preventing Poverty

Anticipate charity by preventing poverty; assist the reduced fellow man, either by a considerable gift or a sum of money or by teaching him a trade or by putting him in the way of business so that he may earn an honest livelihood and not be forced to the dreadful alternative of holding out his hand for charity. This is

the highest step and summit of charity's golden ladder. ~
Maimonides (1135-1204)

-What is particularly proactive about this quote?
-How does this quote provide a foundation for social justice?
-Where are the greatest needs today: close to home, nationally,
internationally?

#15 The Sea Pronounces

The sea pronounces something, over and over, in a hoarse
whisper; I cannot quite make it out. ~ Annie Dillard, Pulitzer
Prize winning author

- Think of times when you enjoyed being by the water.
- Dillard's tone is pensive, searching. Why the yearning?
- How do you respond to life's questions, mysteries?

#16 Know Thyself

Life is a constant challenge to know oneself. ~ Osho

- How well do you know yourself?
- What steps can you take to nurture your self awareness?
- To what extent is self awareness empowerment?

#17 The Medium is the Message

The medium is the message. ~ Marshall McLuhan (1911-1980)

- How do the mass media: newspapers, books, television,
Internet, i Pods, i Phones, video games, movies, social media,
photography, Kindle, etc. vary in their message?
- How are continued innovations in mass media shaping our
culture?

- Which media do you prefer?

#18 Let Go of Searching

As long as you seek for something, you will get the shadow of reality and not reality itself. ~ Shunryu Suzuki (1904-1971)

- Westerners are encouraged to seek and to find. How does this quote turn that notion upside down?
- When did you find the true essence of life when you weren't really looking for it?
- What deceptive shadows lurk in your daily life?

#19 Get Moving

Movement is a medicine for creating change in a person's physical, emotional, and mental states. ~Carol Welch

- How important is exercise to you?
- What form(s) does it take?
- How transformative is exercise in your life?

#20 Fusing Mind and Body

Yoga is bodily gospel. ~Reaven Fields

The yoga mat is a good place to turn when talk therapy and antidepressants aren't enough. ~Amy Weintraub

Tai Chi Chuan, the great ultimate, strengthens the weak, raises the sick, invigorates the debilitated, and encourages the timid. ~Cheng Man Ching

- How much do you know about eastern meditation practices?
- What can the west learn from these perspectives?

- When did you appreciate a quiet moment of reflection with mental and body discipline?

#21 Quick Fixes

There's no quick fix - that's take two aspirins and call me in the morning. ~ Deepak Chopra

- What does Chopra mean in his response to the distressed person?
- In what sense do we live in a culture of quick fixes?
- What kind of counseling might this person need? Where lie the answers?

#22 Silence as Strength

Silence is a source of great strength. ~ Lao Tzu

- Why is silence often difficult to achieve?
- What is true silence?
- How can silence be a great strength?

#23 The Mystery of Hair

If truth is beauty, how come no one has their hair done in a library? ~Lily Tomlin

Those curious locks so aptly twin'd,
Whose every hair a soul doth bind.
~Thomas Carew

Hair brings one's self-image into focus; it is vanity's proving ground. Hair is terribly personal, a tangle of mysterious prejudices. ~Shana Alexander

- Are you having a good hair day?
- What are the attributes of a great hair stylist?
- What's so mysterious about our attitudes to hair?

#24 The Power of a Smile

A smile is a curve that sets everything straight. ~Phyllis Diller

Every time you smile at someone, it is an action of love, a gift to that person, a beautiful thing. ~Mother Teresa

- What does a smile communicate?
- What can a smile accomplish?
- When have you given and received the power of a meaningful smile?

#25 Action is Eloquence

Action is eloquence. ~William Shakespeare

I have always thought the actions of men the best interpreters of their thoughts. ~John Locke

- What actions dominate your day?
- What actions have you admired from others?
- When have you felt that words rang hollow?

#26 Wrestling with Grief

She was no longer wrestling with the grief, but could sit down with it as a lasting companion and make it a sharer in her thoughts. ~George Eliot

- When was the last time that grief overwhelmed you?
- How did you cope with your grief?

- What does Eliot mean when she says that grief can be "a lasting companion?'

#27 Striving for Excellence

Striving for excellence motivates you; striving for perfection is demoralizing. ~Harriet Braiker

- How are striving for excellence and perfection different?
- It's human nature to label or stereotype people. Are you a perfectionist?
- When did you accomplish excellence, something which tested your full powers?

#28 Technology Effects

It has become appallingly obvious that our technology has exceeded our humanity. ~Albert Einstein

- How would you define humanity?
- What technological achievements have been truly devastating to humanity?
- What technological achievements have benefited humanity?

#29 Desire to Acquire

The odds of going to the store for a loaf of bread and coming out with only a loaf of bread are three billion to one. ~Erma Bombeck

- How do stores ensure that you buy more than you planned to?
- How often do you buy on impulse?
- Why is the desire to acquire so strong?

#30 What's on your Night Table?

Always read something that will make you look good if you die in the middle of it. ~P.J. O'Rourke

- You are what you eat, watch, read? How true is this statement?
- Do you prefer fiction or non fiction?
- Will you ever give up living, breathing books for the 'e' variety? i.e. - Kindle, iPad...

#31 Clearing your Mind

A vigorous five-mile walk will do more good for an unhappy but otherwise healthy adult than all the medicine and psychology in the world. ~Paul Dudley White

- Imagine several places where you live where this walk could be very invigorating.
- To what extent do we live in a culture of over the counter fixes?
- How do you like to clear your head?

Chapter 2: February Quotations

#32 Freshly ground heaven

Coffee smells like freshly ground heaven. ~Jessi Lane Adams

- Can you write another simile about coffee which is as good as this one?
- Do you share the author's love for coffee?
- What are your coffee preferences?

#33 Love as habit

Love is an act of endless forgiveness, a tender look which becomes a habit. ~Peter Ustinov

- Is Ustinov overly critical of love?
- What challenges exist for most who are in love?
- How would you describe a mature love?

#34 Wisdom is

He is a wise man (person) who does not grieve for the things which he has not, but rejoices for those which he has. ~Epictetus

- To what extent do you yearn for things which you do not have?
- In what sense is this quote liberating?
- Think about the rejoicing you could do today.

#35 Moving from fears

The linchpin feels the fear, acknowledges it, then proceeds. ~ Seth Godin, Linchpin

- What fears dominate your life?
- How does one best confront those fears?
- How can one resolutely move on and live a vital life?

#36 The patience to wait

*Do you have the patience to wait
till your mud settles and the water is clear?
Can you remain unmoving
till the right action arises by itself? ~Lao-tzu*

- What is the mud that we can stir up for ourselves?

- How do people often respond to those personal dilemmas which arise?
- The repetition of several questions in the quotation encourages introspection. Where lies the wisdom in this quote?

#37 Your children are watching

Don't worry that children never listen to you; worry that they are always watching you. ~Robert Fulghum

- In child raising which age scares you the most?
- What important values do you want to instill within your children?
- The quote distinguishes between words and actions. How can you achieve a balance in your life and example?

#38 The essence of life

What is the essence of life? To serve others and to do good. ~ Aristotle

- How would you have answered the question before seeing the answer?
- Is there some shock value in this statement for a modern reader?
- Reflect on what you can do this upcoming week to live up to the challenge.

#39 Competition in the media

I think it is absolutely essential in a democracy to have competition in the media, a lot of competition, and we seem to be moving away from that. ~Walter Cronkite

- What sources of news and information do you choose to read and watch?
- Is there less competition in the media today?
- How can our democracy and sense of values be threatened by a loss of media diversity?

#40 Friends as healers

The best way to mend a broken heart is time and girlfriends.
~Gwyneth Paltrow

- To what extent do friends help you with emotional hurt?
- Do men need friends as much as women for consolation?
- Think about one good friend you have. How has he/she been integral to your life?

#41 Afraid to be poor?

We have grown literally afraid to be poor. We despise anyone who elects to be poor in order to simplify and save his inner life. If he does not join the general scramble and pant with the money-making street, we deem him spiritless and lacking in ambition. ~William James

- What does it mean to be spiritually poor?
- How can one consciously simplify one's life?
- What is being spiritually rich?

#42 Goals and detours

Establishing goals is all right if you don't let them deprive you of interesting detours. ~Doug Larson

- To what extent may our goals and dreams distract us from daily possibilities?

- What interesting detours is Larson referring to?
- When did you respond to an unexpected opportunity?

#43 Love and change

We are not the same persons this year as last; nor are those we love. It is a happy chance if we, changing, continue to love a changed person. ~W. Somerset Maugham

- How have you changed, matured in the past year?
- Consider how your loved one has changed as well.
- What essential dynamic of love is explored here?

#44 The smallest acts of caring

Too often we underestimate the power of a touch, a smile, a kind word, a listening ear, an honest compliment, or the smallest act of caring, all of which have the potential to turn a life around.~ Leo Buscaglia

- To what extent do you show these smallest acts?
- How can you engage in these loving acts more?
- Think of a time you encouraged someone or someone encouraged you through these small acts?

#45 Seeking acceptance

I did my best, it wasn't much; I couldn't feel so I tried to touch; I've told the truth, I didn't come to fool you. ~Leonard Cohen, 'Hallelujah'

- When have you felt personal insecurity and sought support?
- Where did you find nurture?
- How can people bring joy and strength into their lives?

#46 What is true education?

Education is what remains after one has forgotten what one has learned in school. ~ Albert Einstein

- There is the suggestion that much of schooling isn't really education. Is that overly cynical?
- Think about your experience in school. What do you really remember from the years spent there?
- What valuable lessons have you learned outside of school?

#47 National or global citizen?

I am not an Athenian or a Greek, I am a citizen of the world. ~Socrates

- How can this quote help us to see our relationship with the world?
- What do you like about your own country?
- How can we balance our love for our nation with a love for this world?

#48 Heroes and She-roes

How important it is for us to recognize and celebrate our heroes and she-roes! ~ Maya Angelou

- What are more examples of politically correct expressions?
- To what extent are men and women considered equals in society today?
- Think of she-roes in history, literature, in modern society, in your personal associations.

#49 Ecstasy and agony

For each ecstatic instant/We must an anguish pay/In keen and quivering ratio/ to the ecstasy ~Emily Dickinson

- To what extent do you agree that we 'must' pay an anguish for each ecstasy?
- Is your life a balance of joys and sorrows?
- What is the right mindset in living out one's life?

#50 Visionary alienation

Those who are able to see beyond the shadows and lies of their culture will never be understood, let alone believed, by the masses. ~Plato

- Who were some visionaries of the past?
- Who do you consider a visionary today?
- To what extent do we live in a culture where there is 'the tyranny of the majority'?

#51 Power and responsibility

I think of a hero as someone who understands the degree of responsibility that comes with his freedom. ~Bob Dylan

Remember with great power comes great responsibility. ~ *Spiderman* movie

- What responsibilities should a hero exemplify?
- Who has had great power but shirked his/her responsibilities?
- Reflect upon your own great responsibilities and how well you are fulfilling them.

#52 Wasting time

The time you enjoy wasting is not wasted time. -Bertrand Russell

- Is Russell endorsing procrastination?
- How do you like to waste your time?
- What provides personal enrichment for you?

#53 Questions and answers

It is better to know some of the questions than all of the answers. - James Thurber

- What are some good questions to ask about our modern existence?
- How can your children or students be taught about asking good questions?
- Reflect on one lingering question you have about life.

#54 The cruelest prison

The cruelest prison of all is the prison of an unforgiving mind and spirit. ~Piri Thomas

- How would you distinguish between mind and spirit?
- Why is bitterness particularly destructive?
- How can one resolve to be more forgiving?

#55 Our chief want

Our chief want is someone who will inspire us to be what we know we could be. ~ Ralph Waldo Emerson

- Why is this quote a good one for teachers and parents?
- Did a teacher ever kindle an inspiration within you about your potential?
- How can you apply this quote in your every day life?

#56 Wasted youth

Youth is wasted on the young. *~George Bernard Shaw*

- What do young people take for granted?
- Would you live your youth any differently if you had the chance?
- How do you feel about aging?

#57 Wealth is life

There is no wealth but life. *~John Ruskin*

- If you won a $100,000 lottery, what would you do with the money?
- In what sense does life make one wealthy?
- How does one confront the dominate values of our day?

#58 Kindness in the face of battles

Be kind, for everyone you meet is fighting a hard battle. ~ Plato

- What kind of battles does everyone fight?
- What difficulties have you personally confronted recently?
- When did you show kindness beyond your immediate circle of friends and family?

#59 Finding peace within

If you do not find peace in yourself, you will never find it anywhere else. ~ Paula Bendry

- Where do people look for peace?
- Why is finding personal peace so complex and difficult?
- In what sense have you struggled, and how have you found personal peace?

Chapter 3: March Quotations

#60 Giving as Privilege

Think of giving not as a duty but as a privilege. ~ John D. Rockefeller Jr.

- How does this quote turn the understanding of giving upside down?
- For what blessings are you thankful?
- Reflect on the possible areas where you can provide vital support?

#61 Multi-tasking

He who hunts two hares, leaves one and loses the other. ~ Japanese proverb

- This seems a timely quote these days. To what extent do you multitask?
- Do you agree that often multitasking is counterproductive?
- How can you make changes to your lifestyle to enhance your life and productivity?

#62 Your body as temple

Every man is the builder of a temple called his body. ~ Henry David Thoreau

- What does Thoreau mean that one's body is a temple?
- How well are you taking care of, or nurturing your body?
- To what extent can you use your body for more than self centered interest this week?

#63 Person to person

Do not wait for leaders; do it alone, person to person. ~ Mother Teresa

- How eager are you to take the lead?
- Mother Teresa's gift was dealing with people one at a time. To what extent does her example inspire you?
- Reflect upon your daily relationships and how this quote can affect your actions this week and make you a leader.

#64 Eliminating Non-essentials

The wisdom of life consists in the elimination of non essentials. ~ Lin Yutang

- How busy is your life?
- What are some of the non essentials in your life which may rob you of vitality?
- What are the essentials which you could enrich?

#65 How we spend our lives

Most of us spend our lives as if we had another one in the bank. ~ Ben Irwin

- How do you spend your days?
- Do you feel that some of your time could be better managed?
- Will 'one time around' be enough for you?

#66 Fragility as friendship

Good friendships are fragile things and require as much care as any other fragile and precious thing. ~ Randolph Bourne

- How many good friends do you have?
- How precious are those friends to you?
- How does one cultivate good friendships?

#67 Doing all the talking

Never fail to know that if you are doing all the talking, you are boring somebody. ~ Helen G. Brown

- Are you more a talker or a listener?
- What have you learned about effective communication skills?
- How can you nurture a relationship this week?

#68 Facing problems

Not everything that is faced can be changed, but nothing can be changed until it is faced. ~ James Baldwin

- How good are you at identifying your problems and shortcomings?
- How difficult is it to overcome them?
- What are the benefits/drawbacks of undertaking a self analysis?

#69 Sympathy

There is nothing sweeter than to be sympathized with. ~ George Santayana

- When is the last time you received comfort through sympathy?
- What are the essential dynamics of showing sympathy?

- How can you become a better sympathizer?

#70 Shopping bliss

Whoever said money can't buy happiness simply didn't know where to go shopping. ~Bo Derek

- Reflect upon your shopping experiences.
- Are you increasingly buying items online?
- To what extent is happiness for you defined by acquiring things?

#71 Look like a winner

Regardless of how you feel inside, always try to look like a winner. Even if you are behind, a sustained look of control and confidence can give you a mental edge that results in victory. ~ Arthur Ashe

- Is Ashe overly optimistic here in the power of appearances?
- To what extent do you practice the power of positive thinking?
- Reflect on several acquaintances who exemplify Ashe's quote.

#72 Building character

Character builds slowly, but it can be torn down with incredible swiftness. ~ Faith Baldwin

- Reflect on several strengths of your character.
- When did you find your character tested and diminished?
- How do you find strength to move forward?

#73 Kindness at home

If you have only one smile in you, give it to the people you love.
"Don't be surly at home, then go out in the street and start
grinning 'Good morning' at total strangers. ~ Maya Angelou

- In what sense is this quote ironic?
- How can you characterize yourself around the home and your family?
- Reflect on how this quote can enhance your relationships with family, friends, and outside relationships.

#74 Change

The main dangers in this life are the people who want to change everything or nothing. ~ Lady Nancy Astor

- What are the dangers in each kind of person?
- How would you characterize yourself?
- Reflect on how one should respond to change.

#75 Intention

Others have seen what is and asked why. I have seen what could be and asked why not. ~ Robert F. Kennedy

- What questions do you have about life and society?
- What would you like to see transformed?
- Reflect on one proactive thing you could do this week.

#76 Thought for others

Be unselfish...If you think of yourself only, you cannot develop because you are choking the source of development, which is spiritual expansion through thought for others. ~ Charles Eliot

- Why is it difficult not to be unselfish?
- When did you find satisfaction and personal growth when you thought and acted for others?
- Think of several people whom you could emulate that live up to the quote.

#77 Downsizing

Transformation also means looking for ways to stop pushing yourself so hard professionally or inviting so much stress. ~ Gail Sheehy

- Do you agree with the above quote?
- To what extent do you experience growth as a workaholic?
- What steps could you take to reduce your stress load and focus on things which really matter?

#78 The art of waiting

Waiting is one of the great arts. ~ Margery Allingham

- Think about the different areas and relationships where you could show some patience and wait.
- Have you ever reacted too quickly and regretted your actions?
- How can you turn waiting into an art form?

#79 From thoughts to destiny

Watch your thoughts, for they become words.
Watch your words, for they become actions.
Watch your actions, for they become habits.
Watch your habits, for they become character.
Watch your character, for it becomes your destiny. - unknown

- How are **thoughts, words, actions, habits, character, destiny** tied so closely together?
- It all begins with your thoughts. How can you cultivate your thoughts to get your life going in the right direction?
- Reflect on some of your habits, both negative and positive.
- How will you like to be remembered?

#80 Understanding, a two way street

Understanding is a two-way street. ~ Eleanor Roosevelt

- How well do you get along with people?
- What are the skills which empower communication and understanding?
- Select a person you can try to understand better.

#81 Society as one big family

There can be hope only for a society which acts as one big family, not as many separate ones. ~ Anwar Sadat

- What are the obstacles for greater global harmony?
- What visionary people, locally, nationally, internationally, have helped to create a positive direction?
- Think of one specific way that you can help cultivate more interaction and understanding within your life.

#82 Reconciliation

Reconciliation is more beautiful than victory. ~ Violetta Chamorro

- Think of the times you sought victory over reconciliation. Were you happy with the result? How did it make your 'adversary' feel?

- Why is reconciliation more desirable, yet more difficult?
- What are the necessary steps in conflict resolution?

#83 Security as myth

Security is mostly superstition. It does not exist in nature. ~ Helen Keller

- We know about Helen Keller's insecurities and obstacles in life. What insecurities do we face daily?
- How should we respond to those insecurities?
- How can this quote enrich our daily life?

#84 Creating the self

The self is not something that one finds. It is something one creates. ~ Thomas Szasz

- How would you define your self?
- To what extent have you shaped who you are today?
- What other factors have affected your self?
- What steps can you take to mould your self into new paths?

#85 Coming alive

Don't ask what the world needs. Ask what makes you come alive, and go do it. Because what the world needs is people who have come alive.~ Howard Thurman

- What do you get excited about?
- How can you channel this enthusiasm in positive ways?
- How can you encourage others to do the same?

#86 When we lack experience

I probably hold the distinction of being one movie star who, by all laws of logic, should never have made it. At each stage of my career, I lacked the experience. ~ Audrey Hepburn

- When have you felt under qualified?
- When did a little bit of audacity and courage enable you to succeed?
- To what extent do you believe in yourself?

#87 Today is the most important

Nothing is worth more than this day. ~ Johann Von Goethe

- What transpired in your day yesterday?
- What are your plans for tomorrow?
- Are you living up to Goethe's quote?

#88 Working with limitations

Do what you can, with what you have, where you are. ~ Theodore Roosevelt

- What are several of your limitations?
- To what extent do they compromise your daily life?
- How can you resolve to work with your limitations to get the most out of each day?

#89 True measure of a person

The true measure of a man (person) is how he treats someone who can do him absolutely no good. - Ann Landers

- To what extent do you focus on people who may be useful to you?
- Who are the peripheral people in your life that you may be ignoring?
- How can you enrich the relationships of those around you?

#90 Instilling values

Instill great values in your children today and your grandchildren will prosper tomorrow. - Christy Borgeld

- What are some of the challenges of parenting, including raising teens?
- What values are you trying to instill in your children?
- To what extent do you think that you model the values your parents taught you?

Chapter 4: April Quotations

#91 Happiness and right

If you really want to be happy, always try to do what's right. - Bill Blackman

- Does the 'happiness industry' always reflect what is right?
- What do you consider to be the virtues which cultivate happiness?
- Is the pursuit of happiness a worthy goal all the time?

#92 To succeed

To laugh often and much; to win the respect of intelligent people and the affection of children; to earn the appreciation of honest critics and endure the betrayal of false friends; to appreciate beauty, to find the best in others; to leave the world a bit better, whether by a healthy child, a garden patch or a redeemed social condition; to know even one life has breathed easier because you have lived. This is to have succeeded. ~Ralph Waldo Emerson

- Which of the attributes in Emerson's list are the most meaningful for you?
- How does our society define success?
- How well do you measure up to Emerson's definition of success?

#93 A lifetime

How far you go in life depends on your being tender with the young, compassionate with the aged, sympathetic with the striving, and tolerant of the weak and strong. Because someday in your life you will have been all of these. ~ George Washington Carver

- What does Carver mean "sympathetic with the striving"? Why do they need sympathy?
- Also what does Carver mean by "tolerant of the weak and strong"? Why do they need our tolerance?
- In a nutshell what is Carver's philosophy of life from which we can learn?

#94 Wisdom

Wisdom is oftentimes nearer when we stoop than when we soar.~ William Wordsworth

- To what extent do you practice humility?
- Think of the peripheral people you meet who may provide wisdom if you are open.
- When did you find serendipity in an everyday situation?

#95 Excellence as habit

We are what we repeatedly do; excellence, then, is a habit. ~ Socrates

- Routine may be a negative thing at times, but practice makes perfect. What are you good at?
- Have you ever considered sharing your expertise with someone else?
- How important is sharing your time and perspective with young or older people in your life?

#96 Happiness within

The essence of philosophy is that a man should so live that his happiness shall depend as little as possible on external things. ~ Epictetus

- What external things distract us from true happiness within?
- How difficult is it for you to distance yourself from these things?
- What personally works for you in finding peace?

#97 Spirit of adventure

A good traveller has no fixed plans, and is not intent on arriving. ~ Lao Tzu

- What are the qualities of a great traveller?
- Think about several places which you enjoyed visiting.
- Is Lao Tzu using traveller as a metaphor here? As we travel through life how should we go?

#98 The past as shaper

We can chart our future clearly and wisely only when we know the path which has led to the present. ~ Adlai E. Stevenson

- What have been the chief factors which have influenced your life so far?
- How can you use your past experiences to shape a clear and wise future?
- Reflect on several of the most pivotal experiences of your life.

#99 Focus on the remedy

Don't find fault. Find a remedy. ~ Henry Ford

- When was the last time you complained and found faults with something?
- When did you prove yourself to be quite resourceful and found a remedy?
- Why is Henry Ford such a role model?

#100 Stillness first

One's action ought to come out of an achieved stillness: not to be a mere rushing on. ~ D. H. Lawrence

- What factors in our society encourages us to rush and be in a hurry?
- How does stillness help us to be more measured and creative in our responses?
- How can you try to cultivate more quality, peaceful times in your life?

#101 Gut feeling

A trembling in the bones may carry a more convincing testimony than the dry documented deductions of the brain. ~ Llewelyn Powers

- How often do you let emotions determine your actions?
- Why does Powers suggest that our gut feelings can often be more appropriate than logical expressions?
- Think about a time when a vulnerable and emotional response was very effective.

#102 Humility

Humility is the only true wisdom by which we prepare our minds for all the possible changes of life. ~ George Arliss

- What significant changes have you experienced over the years?
- To what extent have you acquired humility?
- Reflect on the wisdom of being humble.

#103 Survival of the species

It is not the strongest of the species that survive, nor the most intelligent, but the one most responsive to change. ~ Charles Darwin

- What makes life seem like a real struggle?
- To what extent has change impacted your life?
- How have you (or will you) respond to change in effective ways?

#104 Commitment

If you deny yourself commitment, what can you do with life? ~ Harvey Fierstein

- What commitments do you hold dear?
- Have you ever broken a commitment?
- What significant new commitment (resolution) could you begin this week?

#105 Seeing

One may have good eyes and yet see nothing. ~ Italian proverb

- What wonderful sites have you seen? Distant places and near?
- To what extent are you sometimes oblivious to the simple wonders in your life?
- How can you try to be more sensitive to relationships and the needs around you this week?

#106 Our mission

Here is a test to find out whether your mission on earth is finished: If you are alive, it isn't. ~ Richard Bach

- What missions dominate your life?
- Missions may also carry a negative connotation. (Man on a mission.) What preoccupations distract you from what is really important?
- Reflect on your mission statement. Ideally what are your important daily motivations?

#107 Prejudices

A great many people think they are thinking when they are merely rearranging their prejudices. ~ Edward Murrow

- Most people like to think that they are free of prejudices, but let's be honest. What are yours?

- How do these prejudices and personal assumptions affect your life?
- Reflect on how you can be more open and tolerant.

#108 Small things, great love

To show great love for God and our neighbour, we need not do great things. It is how much love we put in the doing that makes our offering something beautiful for God. ~ Mother Teresa

- How well do you know your neighbours?
- What do you really love to do which might be shared with someone else?
- What small things could you do to get to know a neighbour a little better?

#109 Simple cures

A good laugh and a long sleep are the best cures in the doctor's book. ~ Irish Proverb

- When is the last time you had a good laugh? Do you have a good joke at the ready?
- Would you agree that a laugh and sleep are the best cures? What would you add which gives you health and vitality?
- Why is insomnia and sleep disorders quite common in our society?
- Reflect on how you can take better care of your body and psyche.

#110 Walking toward inspiration

If you are seeking creative ideas, go out walking. Angels whisper to people on a walk. ~ Raymond Inmon

- Do you find that walking or exercising helps to energize you?

- What enriching ideas have you gained while the blood is pumping and the air is fresh?
- What other ways work for you in jump starting ideas and gaining inspiration?

#111 Inner worth

No one can figure out your worth but you. ~ Pearl Bailey

- Think about the people who have supported and encouraged you.
- What are some of your accomplishments of which you are proud?
- Ultimately, you are the judge of your true worth. How can you motivate yourself to be the best you can be?

#112 Faith and distance

Faith is the daring of the soul to go farther than it can see. ~ William Newton Clark

- Think about several faiths that you hold dear.
- How have these faiths empowered you?
- What faiths may you want to pursue or cultivate?

#113 Beyond skepticism

The problems of the world cannot possibly be solved by skeptics or cynics whose horizons are limited by the obvious realities. We need people who can dream of things that never were. ~ John F. Kennedy

- Think about several problems in society.
- How do you feel about the skeptics and cynics whom you know?

- How can you use your positive dreams or vision to make a difference in your own small way?

#114 Facing reality

We must have strong minds, ready to accept facts as they are. ~ Harry S. Truman

- What are some of the harsh realities of life?
- To what extent do we attempt to sugarcoat them?
- Think of one reality that you can face more directly.

#115 Life's path

All men (people) should strive to learn before they die, what they are running from, and to, and why. ~ James Thurber

- What are you running from?
- What are you running to?
- Why?

#116 Accepting yourself

To accept ourselves as we are means to value our imperfections as much as our perfections. ~ Sandra Bierig

- OK, none of us is perfect. What are your imperfections?
- And, admit it, you are quite unique and talented. What are you good at?
- To what extent have you accepted yourself and made the best of your strengths and weaknesses?

#117 Open to serendipity

Not knowing when the dawn will come, I open every door. ~
Emily Dickinson

- Serendipity is to be open to the small gifts around us. When was
the last time you experienced it?
- Think of the different sources of serendipity.
- Dawn also may suggest a rebirth, rejuvenation, a divine
revelation, or epiphany. Expand upon how you can become more
open to the dawn.

#118 Expressing all

*It is only by expressing all that is inside that purer and purer
streams come.* ~ *Brenda Ueland*

- Is it possible for you to get everything out?
- How easy is it for you to sort through all of your thoughts
inside?
- Think of ways how you can find expression for your innermost
thoughts so that you can experience wholeness.

#119 Enjoy life

*All animals except man know that the principle business of life is
to enjoy it.* ~ *Samuel Butler*

- To what extent do you enjoy life?
- What hinders you from full enjoyment?
- What steps can you take to get more enjoyment out of life?

#120 Preserve yourself

Endure, and preserve yourself for better things. ~ *Virgil*

- How well are you taking care of your body?
- How well are you holding up to life's challenges?
- Think about the better things which should be pursued.

Chapter 5: May Quotations

#121 Change

We change, whether we like it or not. ~ Ralph Waldo Emerson

- We have all changed physically, but how have you changed in other ways?
- How have these changes affected your perspective on life?
- How can you use these changes to work positively for you?

#122 Courage

Courage is very important. Like a muscle, it is strengthened by use. ~ Ruth Gordon

- Courage is heralded in action movies but also here in quiet ways. When were you courageous?
- And, yet, for most people we fall short in the courage department. With what do you struggle?
- How can you begin in small ways to show more courage?

#123 Don't Wait

You cannot do a kindness too soon, for you never know how soon it will be too late. ~ Ralph Waldo Emerson

- When was the last time someone showed you a kindness?
- When did you last show a kindness?

- Think of several missed opportunities. Can you resolve to show a little more kindness before it's too late?

#124 Questioning yourself

The wise person questions himself, the fool others. ~ Henri Arnold

- How quick are you to judge others?
- To what extent do you truly know yourself?
- Carefully think about several of your values, perspectives, and goals.

#125 Life and onions

Life is like an onion; you peel it off one layer at a time and sometimes you weep. ~ Carl Sandburg

- Think about the layers of your life: personal, social, work, marital, philanthropic...
- Focus on several of your successes, challenges, tears.
- How can you resolve to celebrate your successes and carry forward with hope and confidence?

#126 Opportunities to learn

It is always in season for old men (and women) to learn. ~ Aeschylus

- Think about your learning path. What is your current learning frontier?
- To what extent do newspapers, magazines, books engage your learning?
- What goal can you make about new learning?

#127 Tact

Tact is after all a kind of mind-reading. ~ Sarah Orne Jewett

-Tact is showing careful politeness, a kind of social etiquette.
-How is showing tact like mind reading? What are the signals?
-How can you show more tact in some of your relationships?

#128 Look for good in others

It is a fine thing to have ability, but the ability to discover ability in others is the true test. ~ Elbert Hubbard

- What are several of your special abilities? Did several people help to unlock them for you?
- Now think about several acquaintances. Do you know their gifts?
- How can you help to unlock their gifts?

#129 Living in the past

Living in the past is a dull and lonely business; looking back strains the neck muscles, causes you to bump into people not going your way. ~ Edna Ferber

- Think about several pleasant memories.
- To what extent do you dig up unpleasant memories and experiences?
- Do you agree with Ferber that one should not dwell too much about past events?

#130 On your horizon

A person only grows so much as his horizon allows. ~ John Powell

- How wide is your horizon?
- Describe what you see.
- Where lies growth for you in the short, medium, long term?

#131 Presence over presents

Presence always trumps presents. More than any transient toy, your kids crave time and attention. So let them bask in your attention. ~ Joe Kelly

- To what extent were your parents there for you?
- To what extent did, do, might you spend quality time with your children?
- Reflect on what children truly need.

#132 Making a stand

We know what happens to people who stay in the middle of the road. They get run over. ~ Ambrose Bierce

- To what extent are you a fence sitter? Is that necessarily bad?
- When did you take a decisive stand? Was that a good thing?
- Think of an issue in your life where you could show greater clarity.

#133 Love those who love you

Whatever you do, stamp out abuses, and love those who love you. ~ Voltaire

- Do you show adequate love to those who love you?
- What rude abuses need to be addressed?
- How can you show more compassion today?

#134 Listen to the story

One of the most valuable things we can do to heal one another is listen to each other's stories. ~ Rebecca Falls

- To what extent do you try to apply a quick fix to a problem or cut a conversation short?
- Think of several vivid stories you have heard from someone. Is there therapy in simply listening?
- How can you try to coax out some narrative and introspection from someone this week?

#135 Fresh air, fresh perspective

A vigorous five mile walk will do more good for an unhappy but otherwise healthy adult than all the medicine and psychology in the world. ~ Paul White

- Do you or could you take the opportunity to take some energizing walks?
- Would you agree that a good walk or run is rejuvenating?
- How can you add some recreational spice to your day?

#136 Pardons

We are all full of weakness and errors; let us mutually pardon each other our follies; it is the first law of nature. ~ Voltaire

- To what extent do you hold grudges or show impatience with some people?
- How can you become more forgiving and understanding?
- Think of one specific person with whom you could make amends.

#137 Wanting things

I do not read advertisements. I would spend all of my time wanting things. ~ Franz Kafka

- To what extent does advertising affect your purchases?
- What items do you own that you may not really need?
- How can you simplify and minimize your purchase wish list?

#138 High expectations

High expectations are the key to everything. ~ Sam Walton

- Look where high expectations got the founder, Sam Walton-Walmart! Impressed?
- Think about some of your expectations: personal, family, economic, educational, social, spiritual,...
- Narrow your focus now to one or two specific expectations you can aim for in the short term.

#139 The poison and the sting

I know too well the poison and the sting of things too sweet. ~ Adelaide Proctor

- What in life can be too sweet?
- Why can they bring disappointment or hardship?
- How can one temper too much sweetness in life?

#140 Believing

More persons, on the whole, are humbugged by believing in nothing than by believing in too much. ~ P. T. Barnum

- Are you more an optimist or a pessimist?

- What is your philosophy of life?
- What are some of your firmly held beliefs?

#141 Wilderness of intuition

You have to leave the city of your comfort and go into the wilderness of your intuition. What you'll discover will be wonderful. What you'll discover is yourself. ~ Alan Alda

- What makes you feel comfortable and secure?
- Think of several times when you went outside your comfort zone.
- Think of a way you can experience growth and enrichment.

#142 Forgiving a friend

It is easier to forgive an enemy than a friend. ~ Dorothee Deluzy

- Why might it be easier to forgive an enemy?
- Why might the forgiving process be more difficult for a friend?
- Identify the steps you can use to begin to forgive those in your relationships.

#143 An ounce of help

When a person is down in the world, an ounce of help is better than a pound of preaching. ~ Edward Bulwer-Lytton

- How quick are you to judge, stereotype, and talk about someone else who may be down?
- How do you feel about someone who gives you advice?
- Think of someone who is alienated, alone...who may appreciate a little help from you.

#144 Learning

Learning is a treasure that will follow its owner everywhere. ~ Chinese proverb

- Think of several fond learning experiences you have had.
- What is on your radar at this time to expand your knowledge and skill set?
- Do you have an opportunity to share your learning with someone else?

#145 Living in the moment

The secret of health for both mind and body is not to mourn for the past, not to worry about the future, or not to anticipate troubles, but to live in the present moment wisely and earnestly. ~ Buddha

- What in the past can you try to let go?
- What in the future?
- What can you do in the present to enrich your life and those around you?

#146 The right thing

The truth of the matter is that you always know the right thing to do. The hard part is doing it. ~ Norman Schwarzkopf

- Do you agree that you always know the right thing to do? Is there ever a gray area?
- Why is it sometimes difficult to do the right thing?
- Reflect on how you can do the right thing for yourself or for someone else this week.

#147 A light from within

People are like stained glass windows. They sparkle and shine when the sun is out, but when the darkness sets in, their true beauty is revealed only if there is a light from within. ~ Elisabeth Kubler-Ross

- How well do you mask your true feelings when you are out and about?
- How do you feel about yourself and your life deep within?
- What can you do to nurture a good feeling about yourself and set a positive direction for your life?

#148 A responsibility to care

Provision for others is a fundamental responsibility of human life. ~ Woodrow Wilson

- To what extent do you care for others?
- How can you widen the circle a little more?
- First, how well are you taking care of yourself, the source of the outreach to others?

#149 Gleanings each day

True wisdom lies in gathering the precious things out of each day as it goes by. ~ E. S. Bouton

- Our daily life is a classroom. What did you learn today?
- How sensitive are you to the little insights that surround your daily life?
- How can you gather these treasures and hold them close?

#150 Questions and answers

You can tell whether a man is clever by his answers. You can tell whether a man is wise by his questions. ~ Naguib Mahfouz

- Do you prefer giving answers or asking questions?
- What are several questions you have about life?
- How can you help someone this week by asking some good questions?

#151 Truth and laughter

The absolute truth is the thing that makes people laugh. ~ Carl Reiner

- How does this quote seem ironic?
- When was the last time you had a good laugh? What did the joke reveal about life?
- Think of ways you can lighten up and reflect the vibrancy of life to others.

Chapter 6: June Quotations

#152 Saying it hot

Be still when you have nothing to say; when genuine passion moves you, say what you've got to say, and say it hot. ~ D. H. Lawrence

- Are you generally talkative or more quiet?
- When was the last time you expressed something with passion because you believed in your convictions?
- Interesting that Lawrence uses the word hot. Reflect on what he meant.

#153 Grabbing life

Life loves to be taken by the lapel and told: 'I'm with you, kid. Let's go.' ~ Maya Angelou

- To what extent is your life dominated by planning, preparation, cautiousness?
- How can you resolve to embrace life more actively?
- What are some activities which invite more participation from you?

#154 Just one day

A single day is enough to make us a little larger or, another time, a little smaller. ~ Paul Klee

- What possible actions could you do to make yourself a little larger?
- A little smaller?
- Reflect on the decisions you make each day which make you a little larger, a little smaller.

#155 Work and play

When you're following your energy and doing what you want all the time, the distinction between work and play dissolves. ~ Shakti Gawain

- What activities stimulate your positive energy?
- To what extent does your work reflect your positive energy?
- How can you harness your positive energy in your daily work and play?

#156 Accepting a friend's flaws

Two persons cannot long be friends if they cannot forgive each other's little failings. ~ Jean Bruyere

- Think about several of your closest friends and when they disappointed you.
- How did you react to them and how did it affect your relationship?
- How can you try to forgive little failings and keep your relationship vital?

#157 Mundane tasks

Every job has drudgery... The first secret of happiness is the recognition of this fundamental fact. ~ M. C. McIntosh

- What do you like, dislike about your job, your daily routines?
- How can you accept mundane tasks and turn them into contentment?
- How can you find inner happiness in the valleys and summits of your day?

#158 Growth

Happiness is neither virtue nor pleasure nor this thing nor that but simply growth. We are happy when we are growing. ~ William Butler Yeats

- What is happiness in your mind?
- Yeats suggests it is not a lot of things. To what extent do you agree or disagree?
- Reflect on your growth areas and why they might be very important to pursue them.
- Can you designate a new growth area?

#159 Expressing ourselves

Never express yourself more clearly than you are able to think. ~ Niels Bohr

- How good are your conversational skills?
- To what extent do you talk about things you may not know that much about?
- What main insight can you glean here from Bohr's quotation?

#160 The greatest good

The greatest good you can do for another is not just to share your riches, but to reveal to him his own. ~ Benjamin Disraeli

- What are several of your riches, talents?
- What people in your life helped you to discover and nurture those talents?
- How can you help someone to unlock his/her own talents this week?

#161 Whole-hearted help

Never reach out your hand unless you're willing to extend an arm. ~ Elizabeth Fuller

- Distinguish between talk and action.
- How does one give with one's whole heart?
- Think of several scenarios where you could extend not only your hand but your arm.

#162 Release and grow in love

In hatred as in love, we grow like the thing we brood upon. What we loathe, we graft into our very soul. ~ Mary Renault

- Have you ever been overcome with hate, jealousy, or envy?
- To what extent can these negative feelings consume your vitality?
- How can you find release from this negativity and grow in love?

#163 Adventurous spirit

I feel very adventurous. There are so many doors to be opened, and I'm not afraid to look behind them. ~ Elizabeth Taylor

- When was the last time you felt adventurous?
- How can you cultivate that feeling more often?
- Think about your strengths and how you can build on them.

#164 Sleep and health

Health is the first muse, and sleep is the condition to produce it. ~ Ralph Waldo Emerson

- How can you describe your sleep habits?
- To what extent do you struggle with irregular sleep?
- What proactive steps can you take to ensure that you get adequate and restful sleep?

#165 Prayer as barometer

Prayer at its best is the expression of the total life, for all things else being equal, our prayers are only as powerful as our lives. ~ A. W. Tozer

- How important is prayer to you?
- To what extent might prayer help you to improve the vitality of your life?
- What are the dynamics of good prayer?

#166 Too much close contact

The chain of friendship, however bright, does not stand the attrition of constant close contact. ~ Sir Walter Scott

- Can you get too much of a good thing?
- How do you find the right balance in your relations with friends?
- What are the characteristics of quality time with friends?

#167 Ambition and happiness

When ambition ends, happiness begins. ~ Hungarian Proverb

- To what extent does a desire to get ahead consume your thoughts and efforts?
- Does this quest moderate as one gets older?
- We have been told that ambition is a often a virtue. With what should it be balanced?

#168 Changing perspective

A weed is no more than a flower in disguise. ~ James Lowell

- A dandelion has its day when it is as beautiful as a flower. Why do we want to pull them out?
- How can the weeds in our life carry positive potential?
- Think about your perspective on the positive and negative aspects of life. What does this quote encourage one to do?

#169 Recovering

Suffering isn't ennobling, recovery is. ~ Christiaan Barnard

- How does Barnard put suffering into perspective?
- Think of times when you suffered and you recovered. How did you do it?
- What have you learned through the suffering/recovery process?

#170 Middle of the road

We know what happens to people who stay in the middle of the road. They get run over. ~ Ambrose Bierce

- Do you agree or disagree with this quote?
- What are the benefits of taking a middle position, the drawbacks?
- Think of times when you were a conciliator and times when you took a passionate stand. Perhaps there is room for both actions in our life?

#171 Step into the water

If your ship doesn't come in, swim out to it. ~ Jonathan Winters

- To what extent do you wait for things to happen in your life?
- When did you take the initiative and make something happen?
- Reflect on several opportunities which may provide some exciting possibilities for you.

#172 Actions tell all

Trust only movement. Life happens at the level of events, not of words. Trust movement. ~ Alfred Adler

- To what extent are you making things happen in your life?
- Reflect on several people who exemplify a vital life through their actions.
- Think about the diversity of actions: work, family, friends, community, spiritual, philanthropy, etc.

#173 Response instead of reaction

A life of reaction is a life of slavery, intellectually and spiritually. One must fight for a life of action, not reaction. ~ Rita Mae Brown

- What is the difference between acting and reacting?
- Think of a time when you reacted. How could the situation have been better if you had acted?
- How can you become more proactive in your daily life?

#174 Changing seasons

To be interested in the changing seasons is a happier state of mind than to be hopelessly in love with spring. ~ George Santayana

- What is so lovable about spring?
- Why should we balance our enthusiasm for spring with the other seasons?
- Reflect on the seasons of our lives.

#175 Being gifted

It is one thing to be gifted and quite another thing to be worthy of one's own gift. ~ Nadia Boulanger

- Everyone is gifted. What are your gifts?
- How can one be worthy of the gifts bestowed?

- Think of specific ways you can use several of your gifts wisely.

#176 Compliments

I can live for two months on a good compliment. ~ Mark Twain

- When were you were flattered by a good compliment?
- When did you provide a thoughtful, sincere compliment?
- Think about several people in your life who might benefit from some encouragement.

#177 New endings

Though no one can go back and make a brand new start, anyone can start from now and make a brand new ending. ~ Carl Bard

- What do you wish you could redo if you had the chance?
- Well, that's impossible....now what can you do today to begin a bright future?
- What are the criteria needed to carry forward with hope and resolve?

#178 Goodness

Goodness is easier to recognize than to define. ~ W. H. Auden

- How do you recognize goodness in the actions of some people around you?
- Why is seeing goodness better than defining it?
- How do you define goodness?
- Think about how you can show some goodness this week?

#179 Consistency

Consistency is the last refuge of the unimaginative. ~ Oscar Wilde

- How much do you like routine?
- Would you agree that consistent people are unimaginative?
- Think about how you can add more creativity and dynamism to your life.

#180 Exceeding expectations

I've always tried to go a step past wherever people expected me to end up. ~ Beverly Sills

- Where are you on the pendulum of minimum and maximum effort?
- When did you receive personal satisfaction and recognition for a job well done?
- Think of several opportunities where you could exceed expectations.

#181 This present hour

Gladly accept the gifts of this present hour. ~ Horace

- Which hour is most important for you: past, present, or future?
- What gifts can this present hour bring for you if you are open?
- Think about how you can make the most out of each hour: morning, afternoon, evening.

Chapter 7: July Quotations

#182 Be Somebody

I always wondered why somebody doesn't do something about that. Then I realized I was somebody. ~ Lily Tomlin

- When have you felt frustrated with something in life or in your community which should be done?
- Think about a time when you did something positive in your own small way to make a difference.
- What can you do this week to be somebody?

#183 Change begins in the body

Movement is a medicine for creating change in a person's physical, emotional, and mental states. ~ Carol Welch

- To what extent do you get moving and get that heart pumping throughout the week?
- Would you agree that a good workout affects your emotional and mental states?
- Think about how can you take specific steps (pun here?) to extend your exercise regimen.

#184 A Sense of humour

A sense of humour is part of the art of leadership, of getting along with people, of getting things done. ~ Dwight D. Eisenhower

- To what extent can you let go and laugh at yourself occasionally?
- Good leaders display equanimity, an ability to get along with others, while solving problems and challenges. How much do you have?

- Think about a good and inferior leader. Does this quote ring true?

#185 Aim above morality

Do not be too moral. You may cheat yourself out of much life so. Aim above morality. Be not simply good; be good for something. ~Henry David Thoreau

- Why might morality cheat you "out of much life"?
- What is above morality?
- Think about several things you can do to be "good for something."

#186 Surprises each day

One never knows what each day is going to bring. The important thing is to be open and ready for it. ~ Henry Moore

- How does one prepare to be open and ready for each new day?
- What types of possibilities may exist?
- What area of discovery would you like for this week?

#187 Learning from mistakes

Mistakes are the portals of discovery. ~ James Joyce

- No one likes to make mistakes. Reflect on several.
- Also reflect on several mistakes people around you have made.
- What can you learn or discover about these mistakes?
- How can you respond to people around you who may have made a mistake?

#188 Noble discontent

Noble discontent is the path to heaven. ~ *Thomas Higginson*

-Discontent is often not seen as a virtue. How can it be seen in that light?
- What is the path to heaven?
- How can you turn your discontent into something productive?

#189 Everyone but thyself

Be charitable and indulgent to every one but thyself. ~ *Joseph Joubert*

- This quote counters North American assumptions. How?
- What steps can you take to think less of yourself and more of others?
- Think of several unselfish actions you can take this week.

#190 No friend who never made a foe

He makes no friend who never made a foe. ~*Alfred Lord Tennyson*

- This quote puzzles me. You too?
- Why is having an enemy a good thing as far as friendship goes?
- What human qualities are explored here in the dynamic of friendship?

#191 Light on the water

Happiness is the light on the water. The water is cold and dark and deep. ~ *William Maxwell*

- In what sense is life cold, dark, and deep?

- To what extent is happiness fleeting like light on the water?
- What is Maxwell's perspective on life and happiness?

#192 Thinking and problems

We only think when we are confronted with a problem. ~ John Dewey

-There are petty problems and significant problems. How often do you dwell on small problems.
- Sometimes there are problems beyond our control. To what extent should we be thinking about them?
- Think about a significant problem or challenge which you have right now. How can you solve it well?

#193 Leadership

I have nothing to offer but blood, toil, tears and sweat. ~ Winston Churchill

- To what extent do good leaders lead by example?
- How is a vision propelled by the grit of human experience?
- Think about how you can lead in your own small circle following the example of Churchill?

#194 Hope

Hope is a pleasant acquaintance, but an unsafe friend. ~ Thomas Chandler Haliburton

- Why is it better not to dwell too much on hope?
- What quality is a good friend to have?
- Think about one pleasant hope.

#195 Building confidence

If I am not for myself, who will be? ~ Pirke Avot

- How often do you question your abilities?
- What steps can you take to build up more confidence?
- Think about one anxiety you have and how you can move forward.

#196 Growing up

Growing up is after all only the understanding that one's unique and incredible experience is what everyone shares. ~ Doris Lessing

- What are some of the unique and incredible experiences?
- In education, at home and at school, why is it so important to provide children with some of these experiences?
- What accompanies this realization that everyone has these incredible experiences?

#197 Follow through

The immature mind hops from one thing to another; the mature mind seeks to follow through. ~ Harry A. Overstreet

- How do parents, teachers help children become mature?
- To what extent is a little immaturity good for adults?
- Reflect on how you have followed through on a number of important endeavours.

#198 Always forget

I never forgive, but I always forget. ~ Arthur James Balfour

- This is an interesting counterpoint to forgiveness. What is commendable about the quote?
- To what extent is forgiveness going another step?
- Why might forgiveness not be that important in some situations?

#199 Duty of a doctor

One of the first duties of the physician is to educate the masses not to take medicine. ~ William Osler

- Do you think most physicians agree with this quote?
- Why are so many medicines prescribed these days?
- How proactive are you in avoiding medicines if at all possible?

#200 A good mind

A good mind possesses a kingdom: a great fortune is a great slavery. ~ Seneca

- What kingdom does a good mind possess?
- Why are riches slavery?
- Reflect some more about what a good mind can possess in life which surpasses riches.

#201 Living, dying well

The art of living well and the art of dying well are one. ~ Epicurus

- How does one live well?
- How does on die well?
- Think about how you can enhance your living part.

#202 In touch with deepest emotions

A person buying ordinary products in a supermarket is in touch with his deepest emotions. ~ J. K. Galbraith

- Does this quote surprise you?
- What decisions do you make in a grocery store which connects with your deepest emotions and desires?
- How can you become a smarter shopper with less impulse buying?
- To what extent does advertising affect your shopping decisions?

#203 A great experience

To a great experience one thing is essential- an experiencing nature. ~ Walter Bagehot

- Think about several great experiences you had.
- What mindset, qualities do you need to have to get the most out of a great experience?
- What wonderful experience do you hope to benefit from in the future?

#204 Work is fun

Work is more fun than fun. ~ Noel Coward

- To what extent do you enjoy work which includes doing chores and projects around the house?
- What do you classify as fun?
- How does one achieve a healthy balance?

#205 Role of a writer

A writer is someone who can make a riddle out of an answer.
~Karl Kraus

- Think of a couple of good reads you have had.
- To what extent did they stimulate you to think because they opened up the horizon on an issue or life situation?
- What is your opinion about easy answers?

#206 Become young

It takes a long time to become young. ~ Pablo Picasso

- This is a paradoxical quote. How can becoming old make you young?
- What do the old see that the young cannot?
- What youthful perspectives and activities can you now enjoy?

#207 Work to become

We work to become, not to acquire. ~ Elbert Hubbard

- Of course, work is necessary to pay off the mortgage and all the bills and necessities. To what extent do you need to buy things with your spare money from your labours?
- How might your work enable you to grow?
- Reflect on what skills, perspectives, values you want to acquire through your labours.

#208 Bad/good luck

In bad luck, hold out; in good luck, hold in. ~ German proverb

- How did you feel during a string of bad luck?

- How did you cope?
- How do you interpret the second part of the quotation?

#209 Life is better

Life, however hard, is preferable to the alternative. ~ Aesop

- Do you find life hard?
- How do you surmount life's challenges?
- Think about five aspects in your journey which celebrate LIFE!

#210 Illusion about the past

The illusion that times that were are better than those that are, has probably pervaded all ages. ~ Horace Greeley

- What pleasant memories do you have of your past?
- Do you ever slip into the mindset that the past was better?
- What vital aspects exist within your life today?
- How can you nurture them?

#211 Infinite hope

We must accept finite disappointment, but we must never lose infinite hope. ~ Martin Luther King

- Note the contrast between finite and infinite.
- How does the quote help to add perspective to the disappointments in our lives?
- How important is hope for you in determining your daily well being?

#212 Challenge and controversy

The ultimate measure of a man is not where he stands in moments of comfort and convenience, but where he stands at times of challenge and controversy. ~ Martin Luther King

- How much comfort and convenience do you experience in your life?
- What are several of the challenges and issues which confront you these days?
- How are you responding to these challenges and issues?
- To what extent do you evade some vital issues?

Chapter 8: August Quotations

#213 Fail better

Ever tried. Ever failed. No matter. Try again. Fail again. Fail better. ~ Samuel Beckett

- Beckett suggests that failure happens a lot. Do you agree?
- Persistence appears to be a virtue here. How persistent are you?
- How can one 'fail better'?

#214 Road less travelled

Sometimes the road less traveled is less traveled for a reason. ~ Jerry Seinfeld

- How does Seinfeld poke fun of the biblical and literary allusion?
- To what extent do you take the paths most follow? What are some of those paths?
- What paths have you taken occasionally which are less traveled by others and which show your individuality or convictions?

#215 Success and work

The only place where success comes before work is a dictionary.
~ Vidal Sassoon

- Have you ever achieved success with little work?
- On the other hand, what successes have you enjoyed largely because of your dedication?
- Think of one area where you can work hard to achieve success.

#216 One friend inside

If at the end I have lost every other friend on earth I shall at least have one friend remaining and that one shall be down inside me.
~ Abraham Lincoln

- How much do you love yourself?
- What do you dislike about yourself?
- How can you enrich the vitality and positive qualities that you have within?

#217 Love made visible

Work is love made visible. ~ Kahlil Gibran

- What aspects of your work do you love?
- What products of your work reveal your love for your craft?
- In what areas can you develop a deeper satisfaction?

#218 The greater part of happiness

The greater part of our happiness or misery depends on our dispositions, and not on our circumstances. We carry the seeds of the one or the other about with us in our minds wherever we go. ~ Martha Washington

- What are the personality traits which may encourage happiness?
- To what extent do you have this disposition?
- When have you been troubled by your circumstances? How did you confront them?

#219 Exceed your grasp

Ah, a man's reach should exceed his grasp, Or what's a heaven for? ~ Robert Browning

- To what extent do you extend yourself and build on your skills and perspectives?
- Think about how you can go beyond your comfort levels and routines.
- What heavens have you reached?

#220 What we need

We need hope. We need change. We need experience. We need pens. ~ Jack Donaghy (Alec Baldwin), on 30 Rock

- What several changes would you like to see?
- How has your experience provided perspective to these proposed changes?
- How can you provide a voice to implement these changes?

#221 Patience to wait

Do you have the patience to wait
till your mud settles and the water is clear?
Can you remain unmoving
till the right action arises by itself? ~ Lao-tzu

- How quickly do you react?

- Have you ever benefited by waiting and thinking through your options of response?
- Think about how right actions can come naturally in your life.

#222 Accomplishment

Do not let time pass without accomplishing something. Otherwise you will regret it when your hair turns gray. ~ Yue Fei

- Does the mid life crisis have something to do with this quote?
- Distinguish between accomplishing something and work.
- What are some things you would like to accomplish in the short/mid/long term?

#223 Three things

I have just three things to teach: simplicity, patience, compassion. These three are your greatest treasures. ~ Lao-tzu

-Are you surprised by the list?
- What would you teach?
- How can you incorporate more of the three above in your life?

#224 Doing nothing

Doing nothing is better than being busy doing nothing. - Lao Tsu

- How busy do you consider your lifestyle to be?
- Busyness is implied as bustling about doing insignificant things. How much are you preoccupied with the little things?
- What are the central tenants to quality nothingness?

#225 Don't sweat the small stuff

Ask yourself this question: 'Will this matter a year from now?' ~ Richard Carlson, Don't Sweat the Small Stuff

- What are you fretting about these days?
- How do you handle the small stresses in your life?
- How does Carlson's question help to put your worries in perspective?

#226 Heroism is endurance

Heroism...is endurance for one moment more. ~ George Kennan

- How tired are you emotionally, physically, mentally?
- How does this quote provide one with resolve to move forward?
- Think about some endurance you can show this week.

#227 Seeing in the dark

The dark is light enough. ~ Christopher Fry

- What does Fry mean in this paradoxical quote?
- How can one be thankful for the dark?
- Think about your vitality even in dark times.

#228 Doubts

The only limit to our realization of tomorrow will be our doubts of today. ~ Franklin D. Roosevelt

- What doubts about yourself, the people in your life, the world...do you have?
- How can you transform some of those doubts into more positive feelings?

- Think about how tomorrow will bring possibility unaffected by doubts.

#229 Your little bit of good

Do your little bit of good where you are; it's those little bits of good put together that overwhelm the world. - Bishop Desmond Tutu

-What little bit of good have you done recently?
- What are the needs which exist where you are?
- How can you expand upon your possibilities for goodness this week?

#230 My symphony

To live content with small means;
to seek elegance rather than luxury,
and refinement rather than fashion;
to be worthy, not respectable,
and wealthy, not, rich;
to listen to stars and birds, babes and sages, with open heart;
to study hard;
to think quietly,
act frankly,
talk gently,
await occasions, hurry never;
in a word, to let the spiritual, unbidden and unconscious, grow up through the common
- this is my symphony.
~William Ellery Channing

- Channing's symphony of life includes 12 qualities, actions, perspectives. Reflect on each one.
- Which qualities seem most poignant for you?

#231 Bravery

Bravery never goes out of fashion. ~ William Thackeray

- In what contexts have you seen bravery in your every day life?
- What opportunity for bravery did you personally avoid?
- How can you resolve to show your convictions more resolutely this week?

#232 Keep running

It takes all the running you can do to keep in the same place. ~ Lewis Carroll

- To what extent do you find yourself just keeping your head above water?
- What challenges do you confront?
- How can you resolve to make some progress on those issues?

#233 A stiff upper lip

Keep a stiff upper lip. ~ 19th-century American proverb

-How much do you try to keep your composure?
-What helps to keep you strong and composed?
-How do you balance assurance and self confidence with being honest about your vulnerabilities?

#234 Being miserable

I sometimes try to be miserable that I may do more work. ~ William Blake

- Are you surprised by this quote?

74

- How can frustration encourage one to be more productive?
- How do you overcome challenging times?

#235 Darkness and light

Darkness reigns at the foot of the lighthouse. ~ Japanese proverb

- How much of a lighthouse are you these days?
- What darkness may lurk?
- How do you try to stay focused on the light?

#236 Champions

Champions keep playing until they get it right. ~ Billie Jean King

- Do you sometimes give up if you don't get it right?
- Reflect on the satisfaction you achieved when you did get something right.
- Think of several areas where persistence may result in champion status for yourself.

#237 Change

Change is not made without inconvenience, even from worse to better. ~ Richard Hooker, theologian

- To what extent do you just go with the flow, the status quo? (Hey, I like that little rhyme.)
- Think about when you brought about some change with some sacrifice.
- How can you work toward a little productive change this week?

#238 Rejoice in the present

Let others praise ancient times. I am glad that I was born in these. ~ Ovid, Roman poet

- To what extent do you praise the past and lament the present?
- How can you focus more on the circumstances of your daily life?
- Think about 5 things which causes you to rejoice about the present.

#239 The tragedy of life

The tragedy of life is not so much what men suffer, but rather what they miss. ~ Thomas Carlyle

- What are you missing, neglecting, overlooking in your daily life?
- How can you resolve to enrich several aspects of your daily life?

#240 Bravery

You can't be brave if you've only had wonderful things happen to you. ~ Mary Tyler Moore

- How perfect is your life?
- How can you show a little bravery to overcome several of your challenges?

#241 Experience

Experience is only half of experience. ~ Johann Wolfgang von Goethe

- What is involved with the other half?
- What can you do to make the most of your experiences?

#242 Boldness

I believe we're at our best when we are boldest. ~ Tony Blair

- How easy is it for you to be bold?
- To what extent do you agree with this quote?
- Think about several contexts in which you can be more bold in an effective way.

#243 Help yourself

God helps those who help themselves. ~ Benjamin Franklin

- How resourceful and forthright are you?
- How can you nurture and develop your independence a little more?
- To what extent do we need to balance independence with care for others?

Chapter 9: September Quotations

#244 It won't be easy

Nobody ever said it would be easy - and that was an understatement. ~ George Mitchell

- When did you find success after considerable difficulty?
- When did you find disappointment, failure after trying very hard?
- What resolution can you make about trying?

#245 Face to the sunshine

Keep your face to the sunshine and you cannot see the shadow. ~ Helen Keller

- What shadows lurk in your life?
- How do you try to stay optimistic despite difficulties?
- How can you bring more sunshine to your life?

#246 Our common dispositions

To complain of the age we live in, to murmur at the present possessors of power, to lament the past, to conceive extravagant hopes of the future, are the common dispositions of the greatest part of mankind. ~ Edmund Burke

- How much do you complain about life and leaders, lament the past, have extravagant hopes?
- Are these qualities negative attributes?
- What several attributes should be the greatest part of mankind?

#247 Put up with the rain

The way I see it, if you want the rainbow, you gotta put up with the rain. ~ Dolly Parton

- What rains shower down on you?
- How do you try to keep dry?
- What rainbows have you seen amidst the challenges, disappointments?

#248 One's actions

The end of man is an action and not a thought, though it were the noblest. ~ Thomas Carlyle

- Think about how your actions can be the most noble thing you do.
- What actions in particular are important?

- How often do you think, but not act? Is that necessarily bad?

#249 Our defects

We succeed in enterprises which demand the positive qualities we possess, but we excel in those which can also make use of our defects. ~ Alexis de Tocqueville

- What positive qualities do you possess?
- What are your defects, weaknesses?
- How can you use a defect to win success? (The idea seems paradoxical.)

#250 Imagination

You cannot depend on your eyes when your imagination is out of focus. ~ Mark Twain

- How much do you use your imagination?
- How have you used your imagination to formulate a vision?
- Use your imagination this week to help you to see your life a little more clearly.

#251 Inner peace

We can never obtain peace in the world if we neglect the inner world and don't make peace with ourselves. World peace must develop out of inner peace. ~ Dalai Lama

- How difficult is it for you to find inner peace?
- How does one try to cultivate and nurture it?
- How can you help to bring peace to those around you?

#252 Plan ahead

Plan ahead or find trouble on the doorstep. ~ *Confucius*

- What different kinds of planning are there?
- In what areas is planning most important?
- What trouble would you like to try and avoid?

#253 The answer

At the center of your being you have the answer;
You know who you are and you know what you want. ~ *Lao-tzu*

- Who are you?
- What do you want?
- What steps will you take to achieve what you want?

#254 Peace leads to service

So if we have the habit of being peace, Then there is a natural
tendency for us to go in the direction of service. ~ *Thich Nhat*
Hanh

- Do you exemplify a habit of peace?
- How much service do you provide?
- What area of service could you begin?

#255 True and beautiful words

True words are often not beautiful, just as beautiful words are
often not true. ~ *Japanese proverb*

- What is the central point here?
- Where lies beauty?
- How can you live so that you are an inspiration to others?

#256 The ultimate path

The ultimate path is without difficulty. Just avoid picking and choosing. ~ Sengstan

- How can one best proceed on the path of life?
- What path are you on?
- Reflect on the steps you will take day by day.

#257 Practice compassion

If you want others to be happy, practice compassion. If you want to be happy, practice compassion. ~ Dalai Lama

- When did you last bring happiness to someone?
- How can you cultivate more happiness within yourself?
- How can you reach more beyond self?

#258 Enough

Enough is great riches. ~ Danish proverb

- How much is enough?
- Reflect on the riches of your life.
- How can you devalue your quest for money riches?

#259 All things excellent

All things excellent are as difficult as they are rare. ~ Benedict de Spinoza

- Where have you seen excellence?
- What is required to achieve excellence?
- What excellence have and will you achieve?

#260 Living

I have some problems with my life, but living is the best thing they've come up with so far. ~ Neil Simon

- What problems do you have in your life?
- How can simply living help to address them?
- What are the important ingredients for vital living?

#261 Following

The last camel of the caravan has the same pace as the first. (African proverb)

- Do you like to take the lead?
- What does this proverb suggest about being a follower?
- Reflect on leading and following and what kind of balance is best for you.

#262 Start at the top

When you sweep the stairs, you start at the top. (German proverb)

- What are several of your weaknesses which you would like to sweep into the dust bin?
- Starting at the top, what is your most significant one?
- What can you do to give your life a bit of a boost?

#263 The rush of feelings

Feelings are much like waves; we can't stop them from coming but we can choose which ones to surf. ~Jonaton Martensson

- What feelings, both positive and negative, dominate your last several days?
- To what extent do you let the negative feelings encompass you?
- How can you try to let the positive feelings dominate?

#264 Infinity of nature

I thank you God for this most amazing day, for the leaping greenly spirits of trees, and for the blue dream of sky and for everything which is natural, which is infinite, which is yes. ~e.e. cummings

- What are you thankful for today?
- What in nature have you cherished, enjoyed recently?
- Reflect on the infinite dimensions of nature in your life.

#265 Desperation

The mass of men lead lives of quiet desperation. ~Henry David Thoreau

- How much anxiety do you have about life?
- What are the sources of this anxiety?
- What steps can take to reduce this anxiety level and enjoy your daily life more?

#266 The why and how

He who has a why to live can bear almost any how. ~Friedrich Nietzsche

- What is your why for living?
- What is your why for living? (Yes, think this question through.)
- How does your why help you through the challenges and difficulties?

#267 Choices

Life is the sum of all your choices. ~Albert Camus

- Reflect on the many choices you make in life.
- What choices are you happy about; what choices sad?
- How can you resolve to enhance your life with good choices.

#268 Exercise

Lack of activity destroys the good condition of every human being, while movement and methodical physical exercise save it and preserve it. ~Plato

- How do you exercise?
- What can you do to enhance your exercise regiman?
- What other steps can you take to enhance your physical health?

#269 Knowledge and wonder

The larger the island of knowledge, the longer the shoreline of wonder. ~Ralph W. Sockman

- What areas of knowledge do you pursue?
- How have your pursuits enhanced your understanding and appreciation?
- What new area of learning would you like to pursue?

#270 Kindness and courage

Life is mostly froth and bubble,
Two things stand like stone,
Kindness in another's trouble,
Courage in your own.

~Adam Lindsay Gordon

- When have you shown kindness to someone in trouble?
- How courageous are you in the face of your personal problems?
- To what extent do you try to raise yourself above the "froth and bubble?"

#271 I will prevail

I believe that man will not merely endure: he will prevail. ~ William Faulkner

- To what extent do you 'endure' your life?
- Think about how you will not only endure, but PREVAIL!

#272 Laughter

He who laughs, lasts! ~ Mary Pettibone Poole

- How is your sense of humour?
- How do you try to cultivate it?
- What makes humour a vital ingredient for life?

#273 Common bonds

We will need to remind ourselves, despite all our differences, just how much we share: common hopes, common dreams, a bond that will not break. ~ Barack Obama

- What differences do you see in the people and cultures around you and in the world?
- What hopes do all people have? What dreams?
- How does this quote affect your perspective and actions?

Chapter 10: October Quotations

#274 Hope

Hope is the power of being cheerful in circumstances which we know to be desperate. ~ G.K. Chesterton

- To what extent do you see desperation in your life?
- What enables you to stay positive?
- What several hopes seem worthy to have?

#275 No doubt

Ten thousand difficulties do not make one doubt. ~ John Henry Newman

- What difficulties do have in your life at this time?
- To what extent do you doubt your actions?
- How can you resolve to carry forward with reasonable optimism and trust?

#276 Dare mighty things

Far better it is to dare mighty things, to win glorious triumphs, even though checkered by failure, than to take rank with those poor spirits who neither enjoy much nor suffer much, because they live in the gray twilight that knows not victory nor defeat. ~ Theodore Roosevelt

- How cautious, reticent are you in living out your life?
- When did you try something daring but failed?
- How can you resolve to be a little more bold in meeting life's challenges?

#277 Thin ice

In skating over thin ice, our safety is our speed. ~ Ralph Waldo Emerson

- What aspects of your life do you consider fragile?
- How can Emerson's metaphor help you to gain some strength?

#278 The greatest happiness

My greatest happiness consists precisely in doing nothing whatsoever that is calculated to obtain happiness. ~ Chuang-tzu

- How is this quote paradoxical?
- Think about all the schemes which promise happiness.
- Think about the happiness in nothing.

#279 Knowing oneself

Life is a constant challenge to know oneself. ~ Osho

- How well do you know yourself?
- How is this process a life long process and challenge?
- What key understandings have you reached about yourself?

#280 Nonviolence

For me, nonviolence is not a mere philosophical principle. It rules my life. It is the rule and breath of my life. It is a matter not of the intellect but of the heart. ~ Mahatma Gandhi

- To what extent is the principle of nonviolence important to you?
- How can you enrich the concept in your daily life and perspectives?
- How can you cultivate nonviolence in your heart?

#281 Money

Money doesn't talk, it swears. ~ Bob Dylan

- How can one see money as a dirty word?
- How has money twisted and distorted the beauty of life?
- What can you do to devalue the importance of money in your life?

#282 Life's Tragedies

In this world there are only two tragedies. One is not getting what one wants, and the other is getting it. ~ Oscar Wilde

- What are several things you desperately want but have not received?
- Think about several things you really wanted and then received.
- Why is acquiring something you wished for a tragedy?
- How does one lessen tragedy in one's life?

#283 Complexity

I prefer complexity to certainty, cheerful mysteries to sullen facts. ~ Claude T. Bissell

- Why is complexity more desirable than certainty?
- Cheerful mysteries to sullen facts?
- How can you strive to cultivate more complexity and mystery to your life?

#284 Happiness

Happiness depends on being free, and freedom depends on being courageous. ~ Thucydides

- How free are you?
- What conditions may restrict you?
- How can a little courage enable you to enjoy more freedom?
- Do you fully agree with the quotation?

#285 Winning

It is best to win without fighting. ~ Sun Tzu

- How can one avoid the fight?
- What are the conditions necessary to win?
- How can you win more in your associations without the fight?

#286 Hard times

Can anybody remember when times were not hard, and money was not scarce? ~ Ralph Waldo Emerson

- What do you consider hard about your life?
- How challenged are you with your finances?
- What is Emerson suggesting here about the human condition?

#287 Being human

There will come a day for each of us, more or less sad, more or less distant, when we must accept the condition of being human. ~ Jean Anouilh

- What are we reluctant to accept about being human?
- What are the criterion of being human?
- How might this acceptance be an enrichment for our lives?

#288 Going beyond

To go beyond is as wrong as to fall short. ~ Confucius

- Does this quote counter prevailing opinion of doing more than what is expected?
- How often do you fall short?
- How can you achieve a proper balance in all your efforts?

#289 Know your nature

A person who knows his own nature will know heaven. ~ Mencius

- How well do you know yourself?
- How can truly knowing yourself make you more content about life?
- Identify several specific qualities about yourself which are important to cultivate.

#290 Inexpressible

In truth, all things are inexpressible, empty, calm, and pure. ~ Nagarjuna

- How often do you want to express what you think is true?
- Think about truth as inexpressible where there is calmness and purity.
- What is the nature of truth?

#291 Fortune

Fortune takes nothing away but what she also gave. ~ Roman proverb

- To what extent do you believe in good luck and fortune?
- Why might it be more desirable not to think too much about fortune?
- In the end what should you count on? What is important?

#292 Suffering

If suffer we must, let's suffer on the heights. ~ Victor Hugo

- How much have you suffered?
- What does Hugo mean by suffering "on the heights?"
- Why is exalted suffering a good thing?

#293 Striving

It is better to wear out than to rust out. ~ Richard Cumberland

- In what area(s) are you using your talents well?
- Where do you think you could extend yourself more?
- How can you motivate someone around you to 'bump it up a couple of notches?'

#294 Optimism vs Pessimism

In these times you have to be an optimist to open your eyes when you wake in the morning. ~ Carl Sandburg

- Are you more an optimistic or pessimistic person?
- Where lies reason to be optimistic in the morning?
- What about life provides you with some pessimism?
- How does one cultivate an optimistic life?

#295 Sorrow

It is wrong to sorrow without ceasing. ~ Homer

- Reflect on several major times of sorrow.
- How quickly did you want to carry on with your life?
- How does one best deal with grief?

#296 Failure

Our business in this world is not to succeed, but to continue to fail, in good spirits. ~ Robert Louis Stevenson

- How does this quote surprise you?
- Part of life seems to be acceptance of what comes, both good and bad. How good are you with acceptance?
- The quote also implies that we continue to strive and confront challenges even though we might fail. Where can you show some daring?

#297 Discontent

Discontent is want of self-reliance; it is infirmity of will. ~ Ralph Waldo Emerson

- How often are you plagued with discontent?
- What do you fret over?
- How can you become more self-reliant with purpose and will?

#298 A fighter

They underestimated me, because I am a fighter and not a quitter. ~ Peter Mandelson

- Are you more a fighter or a quitter?
- How does one build a resolve to be a fighter?
- What is the difference between a bad fighter and a good fighter?

#299 Finding contentment

Better the cottage where one is merry than the palace where one weeps. ~ Chinese proverb

- How can too much wealth bring unhappiness?
- How difficult is it for you to simplify your life with fewer expectations?
- When have you felt release and contentment?

#300 Are you a hero?

Everyone is necessarily the hero of his own life story. ~ John Barth

- How are you progressing with your life story?
- How can (do) you overcome the many challenges surrounding your life?
- What are the distinguishing qualities of you as hero?

#301 Fairness

Be fair with others, but keep after them until they're fair with you. ~ Alan Alda

- How much does your own self interest interfere with your fairness to others?
- Exactly what does it mean to be fair?
- How do you get people to be fair with you?

#302 Existence and opportunity

You are born with two things: existence and opportunity, and these are the raw materials out of which you can make a successful life. ~ Charles Templeton

- How do you cultivate and enrich your existence?
- What are several of your strengths and interests?
- How can you use these gifts to take advantage of opportunity?

#303 End of the rope

When you get to the end of your rope, tie a knot and hang on. ~ Franklin D. Roosevelt

- When have you felt recently that you are at the end of your rope?
- How can, do you maintain resolve to carry on?
- What are the tiny silver linings in your life which provide that glimmer of hope?

#304 Facial charm

I think your whole life shows in your face and you should be proud of that. ~ Lauren Bacall

- What do your facial features reveal about your life?
- Do we need to show a perpetual smile or what are the options?
- OK, it's time to feel proud. What about your life is wonderful?

Chapter 11: November Quotations

#305 Joy

What did you think, that joy was some slight thing? ~ Mark Doty

- What several joys have you experienced recently?
- To what extent did you cherish and nurture those joys?
- How does joy fit into the grand scheme of life?

#306 Happiness

Happiness is a conscious choice. ~ Mildred Barthel

- To what extent has the media and our modern day perspectives affected our pursuit of happiness?
- How does one allow happiness to happen?
- How does one fit happiness in the grand scheme of life?

#307 Life

Life isn't all beer and skittles. ~ Thomas Hughes

- Do beer and skittles work for you? What are yours?
- To what extent do you bring play and frivolity into your life?
- How do you try to seek a balance between work and leisure?

#308 Nature's renewal

To cherish was remains of the Earth and to foster its renewal is our only legitimate hope of survival. ~ Wendall Berry

-How much has the earth changed in the last two hundred years?
-Where have you enjoyed nature's splendour?
-What small steps can you take to help to foster its renewal?

#309 Kind relief

Can I see another's woe, and not be in sorrow too? Can I see another's grief, and not seek kind relief? ~ William Blake

- Where have you see human hurt?
- How have you responded in the past?
- What small step can you take to enrich your involvement?

#310 What we give up

It is not what we take up, but what we give up, that makes us rich. ~ Henry Ward Beecher

- There is a paradox in this quote. How can giving something up make one rich?
- When did you decide not to buy an extravagant item which freed up your finances?
- What else could you give up (other than material items) which could provide liberation?

#311 The child

The most important question in the world is, "Why is the child crying?" ~ Alice Walker

- What children of your own or others have you heard cry?
- How good are you in responding to the needs of children?
- Why, according to Walker, is this the most important question of life?

#312 Are you sunshine?

Some people are so much sunshine to the square inch. ~ Walt Whitman

- How much sunshine do you spread?
- Think of a particularly cheerful person whom you know. How does he/she do it?
- How can you resolve to cheer up some person's life today?

#313 Boiling point

We boil at different degrees. ~ Ralph Waldo Emerson

- What is your boiling point?
- How much heat, pressure, difficulty can you withstand?
- How can you resolve to be more calm and tolerant with everything that is going on in your life?

#314 Sense of wonder

If you enjoy living, it is not difficult to keep the sense of wonder.
~ Ray Bradbury

- How much do you enjoy living?
- What's, possibly, holding you back?
- Where have you experienced a sense of wonder recently?
- How can you cultivate more of this sense?

#315 Doing your best

Doing your best at this moment puts you in the best place for the next moment. ~ Oprah Winfrey

- Where in your life are you doing your best?
- To what extent have you experienced satisfaction and success in this pursuit?
- How do you overcome frustration to carry on?

#316 Mistakes

Mistakes are the portals for discovery. ~ James Joyce

- No one likes to think about mistakes. How painful have some been for you?
- To what extent have some mistakes disillusioned you?
- What growth or discoveries have you made over the years from failure?

#317 Success

Success usually comes to those who are too busy to be looking for it. ~ Henry David Thoreau

- What occupies much of your time?
- What different kinds of success may Thoreau be suggesting?
- Is the quote still applicable for people in 'retirement?'

#318 Talk

Don't talk unless you can improve the silence. ~ Jorge Luis Borges

- Communication is a good thing. How can some talk be considered negative?
- When have you been enriched by silence?
- What direction does this quote provide about conversation?

#319 Ease one's pain

If I can stop one heart from breaking, If I can ease one pain, then my life will not have been in vain. ~ Emily Dickinson

- When have you helped someone in emotional distress?
- Why is this quote difficult to follow for some?
- How can you resolve to be a little more of a care giver?

#320 Pain, thought, wisdom

Pain makes man think. Thought makes man wise. Wisdom makes life endurable. ~ John Patrick

- What kind of pain is most difficult?

- What's the difference between thought and wisdom?
- Where have you find wisdom and how has it provided you with hope and courage?

#321 Complaints are a bore

Much in life cannot be affected...but must be borne...without complaint, because complaints are a bore...and undermine the serenity essential to endurance. ~ Dean Acheson

- What aspects of life cannot be affected or changed?
- How much do you complain?
- How can you cultivate more serenity in your life which leads to endurance?

#322 Keep rowing

Everyone must row with the oars he has. ~ Dutch proverb

- How is your rowing going lately?
- Do you have good oars?
- Why is it desirable not to compare our rowing with others?

#323 Fears

There is no such thing as bravery- only degrees of fear. ~ John Wainwright

- What are the different sources of fear in your life?
- How fearful are you in confronting some of your challenges?
- How can you resolve to continue to be 'brave?'

#324 Stumbling

I left the room with silent dignity, but caught my foot in the mat.
~ George Grossmith, English comedian

- How much do you try to look good in front of others?
- How's your sense of humour and being able to laugh at yourself?
- How should we live out our lives in association with others?

#325 Wisdom

An optimist is a person who sees a green light everywhere, while the pessimist sees only the red stoplight. The truly wise person is colorblind. ~ Albert Schweitzer

- Are you more an optimist or a pessimist?
- To what extent do you get excited or disappointed by the green and red lights in your life?
- How can one cultivate and enrich colorblindness in life?

#326 Bet on yourself

The best bet is to bet on yourself. ~ Arnold Glasow

- Where have you placed some good bets,... and some bad bets?
- Why is it a good idea to focus on yourself and try to cultivate your full potential?
- Think about one specific bet you can place on yourself and win.

#327 Change lies within

I've never met a person, I don't care what his condition, in whom I could not see possibilities. I don't care how much a man may consider himself a failure, I believe in him, for he can change the thing that is wrong in his life anytime he is prepared and ready to do it. Whenever he develops the desire, he can take away from his life the thing that is defeating it. The capacity for reformation and change lies within. ~ Preston Bradley

- To what extent do you see the worth or potential in every person you meet?
- How can you help to encourage and motivate someone to be his/her best?
- How can this quote help you to change and grow?

#328 Up to you

I am my own heaven and hell. ~ J.C.F. von Schiller

- When have you made for yourself a heaven?
- When have you made for yourself a hell?
- To what extent can you banish hell from your life?
- What are the steps needed to cultivate a heaven?

#329 At our core

I think we all have a core that's ecstatic, that knows and that looks up in wonder. We all know that there are marvelous moments of eternity that just happen. We know them. ~ Coleman Barks

- To what extent do you have joy at your core?
- How much wonder do you experience in your life?
- How can you cultivate more joy and wonder in your life?

#330 Seeing the world

We must learn to see the world anew. ~ Albert Einstein

- How youthful are your perspectives?

- How can you cultivate and enrich these perspectives?
- Think about several times when you experienced the thrill of being alive.

#331 Home

Without leaving my house, I know the whole universe. ~ Lao-Tsu

- How content are you within your own home and community?
- What truths can you see there which you may be missing?
- How can you cultivate more contentment in your daily life?

#332 Trials

The secret of happiness is not discovered in the absence of trials, but in the midst of them. ~ Ted Nace

- What trials do you currently face?
- How can you turn a challenge into something energizing and rewarding?
- Think about some happiness you hope to gain this week?

#333 True success

To travel hopefully is a better thing than to arrive, and the true success is to labour. ~ Robert Louis Stevenson

- How are you proceeding on the road of life?
- What makes your daily road trip a rewarding pursuit?
- In what labours do you hope to find success?

#334 Hard with yourself

The most intelligent men, like the strongest, find their happiness where others would find only disaster: in the labyrinth, in being hard with themselves and with others, in effort; their delight is in self-mastery; in them asceticism becomes second nature, a necessity, an instinct. ~Friedrich Nietzche

- In what sense is life a labyrinth?
- How hard are you on yourself in your pursuits?
- How can you resolve to be more focused and rigorous?

Chapter 12: December Quotations

#335 Doing without

How many things I can do without! ~ Socrates

-How does this quote contrast with dominant social values?
-To what extent do you pamper yourself and buy extravagant or peripheral items?
- How can you resolve to live with less? Think about several specific ways.
- How might more simplicity and minimalism enrich your life?

#336 Anger

He who angers you conquers you. ~ Elizabeth Kenny

- How easily angered are you?
- How can you resolve to control your anger more?
- What can take the place of anger to put you more in control and more at peace?

#337 Worry

Worry is like a rocking chair; it will give you something to do, but it won't get you anywhere. ~Anonymous

- How much are you prone to worry?
- What steps can you take to reduce worry?
- What is more productive than worry?

#338 Acting foolishly

It is human nature to think wisely and act foolishly. ~ Anatole France

- This site espouses a lot of wisdom with the quotes. (It's easier said than done.) How prone are you to say, think one thing and do the other?
- What foolish things have you done even when you knew better?
- How can you resolve to practice more than preach?

#339 Small deeds done

Small deeds done are better than great deeds planned. ~ Peter Marshall

- How often are you thinking/dreaming about doing great things?
- To what extent do you like to focus on the tasks at hand and doing them well?
- How can you resolve to enrich your daily life?

#340 Friendship as an art

Friendship is an art, and very few persons are born with a natural gift for it. ~ Kahleen Norris

- What are the challenges in building close friendships?
- What are the qualities and nuances of being a good friend?
- How can you resolve to enrich several of your relationships?

#341 Obstacles as guides

The obstacle is the path. ~ Zen proverb

- To what extent do you like to stretch yourself into new areas of learning and discovery?
- What growth have you experienced recently through the challenges of your day?
- What questions do you have at the moment which may help to direct your path?

#342 One day at a time

Home wasn't built in a day. ~ Jane Ace

- How impatient are you in completing projects around the home?
- How do you feel about relations in your family?
- How can you resolve not to fret too much about both and focus on the quality of your daily life?

#343 The best persuasion

The most effective persuasion is a life well lived. ~ Anna Bjorklund

- Our actions speak louder than words or theories. To what extent do you live what you preach?
- How would you describe the quality of your life?
- What can you do to enrich the quality of your daily life?

#344 Knowing yourself

Ninety percent of the world's woe comes from people not knowing themselves, their abilities, their frailties, and even their real virtues. ~ Sydney J. Harris

- As we age, do we get to know ourselves better?
- What are your abilities?
- What are your frailties?
- What are your virtues?
- How can you use this knowledge to enhance the quality of your life?

#345 Being humane

The first condition of humaneness is a little humility and a little diffidence about the correctness of one's conduct and a little receptiveness. ~ Mahatma Gandhi

- How much humility is in your bones?
- How much diffidence (shyness)?
- How prone are you to judge others?
- How receptive are you to the potential of anyone you meet?

#346 Desires

When all the desires that surge in the heart are renounced, the mortal becomes immortal. ~ The Upanishads

- What different desires are there? ....
- How difficult is it for you to release them from your heart?
- Why is absence of desires such an important goal?

#347 The beautiful path

...The beautiful path is patient, always waiting for you to come back, that path that is so familiar to you, and so faithful. It knows you will come back one day, and it will welcome you back. The path will be as fresh and as beautiful as the first time. Love never says that this is the last time. ~ Thich Nhat Hanh

- What is the beautiful path in your life?
- What causes you to stray from that path occasionally?
- How can you resolve to return to that path which lovingly awaits your return?

#348 Love first

I don't want to live- I want to love first and live incidentally. ~ Zelda Fitzgerald

- How much love is in your reservoir?
- To what extent is it difficult for you to show that love to people around you?
- How can you resolve to show more love?
- How can living a life of love add quality to your day?

#349 Inner radiance

Beauty is a radiance that originates from within and comes from inner security and strong character. ~ Jane Seymour

- How secure do you feel within?
- How strong is your character?
- What vulnerabilities, insecurities lurk?
- How can you build up your inner security and find more confidence in your potential?

#350 Making up your mind

Most folks are about as happy as they make up their minds to be. ~ Abraham Lincoln

- How much contentment permeates your life?
- What are the obstacles to finding satisfaction and peace?

- How can you make up your mind to feel more contented and happy with your life?

#351 New every day

We are new every day. ~ Irene Claremont de Castillego

- What shadows of your past linger?
- How discouraged do you feel at times?
- How can this quote give you motivation to find new hope, meaning, and contentment with each new day?

#352 Don't complain

Weep, but don't complain. ~ Dag Hammarskjold

- When have you grieved recently?
- How can weeping be a restorative?
- How can you resolve to complain less?

#353 Humour

Humor is just another defense against the universe. ~Mel Brooks

- What weighs you down about the world, about your life?
- How can you strive to achieve a balance between seriousness and lightheartedness?
- Where do you find release?

#354 The road of life

The road up and the road down are one and the same.
~Heraclitus, Greek philosopher

- Coming and going, waking and sleeping, working and resting, meeting challenges and conquering them, greeting and parting....How should we see life in all its diversity?
- What mind set will enable you to find steadiness and vitality in your daily life?

#355 Cheerfulness

Cheerfulness keeps up a kind of day-light in the mind, and fills it with a steady and perpetual serenity. ~ Joseph Addison

- How cheerful are you generally?
- How do you try to be cheerful amidst challenges in your life?
- How can this quote bring more serenity to your life?

#356 Being discouraged

One of the things I learned the hard way was that it doesn't pay to get discouraged. ~ Lucille Ball

- Interesting that such a brilliant comedian experienced discouragement. When have you felt discouraged?
- How does one overcome discouragement to carry on?

#357 Starting over

We have it in our power to begin the world over again. ~ Thomas Paine

- How realistic is Paine in his proclamation?
- How can we begin the process in the small spaces of our every day lives?
- What kind of vitality can you bring to your daily life?

#358 The right time

Very few things happen at the right time, and the rest do not happen at all. ~ Herodotus

- What do you wish would happen in your life?
- When have you felt discouraged that events didn't happen as you had hoped?
- What perspective is encouraged here about what life brings to us?

#359 Searching

I am searching for that which every man seeks - peace and rest. ~ Dante Alighieri

- How much is your life involved with searching?
- Where can you find peace?
- Where can you find rest?

#360 Smile

Every time you smile at someone it is an action of love, a gift to that person, a beautiful thing.
Mother Theresa

- When was the last time someone gave you a sincere smile?
- How ready are you with your smile for the people you meet?
- How can the smile enrich your life in a comprehensive way?

Sometimes your joy is the source of your smile, but sometimes your smile can be the source of your joy.
Thich Nhat Hanh

- What is the source of your smile which can bring you joy?

- How can you enrich this inner source of vitality in the coming new year?

#361 Being yourself

To be yourself in a world that is constantly trying to make you something else is the greatest accomplishment. ~ Ralph Waldo Emerson

- How has the world tried to shape you?
- How do you resist this shaping influence?
- Think about what makes you distinctive and individual. How can you be more confident in being yourself in your daily life?

#362 Ruined by praise

We would rather be ruined by praise than saved by criticism. ~ Norman Vincent Peale

- What praise have you received? How did you feel?
- What criticism? How did you feel?
- How can criticism have a silver lining?

#363 Subdue appetites

Subdue your appetites and you've conquered human nature. ~ Charles Dickens

- Besides our appetite at the table, what other appetites afflict us?
- To what extent can these appetites distract and adversely affect our lives?
- How can you resolve to subdue these appetites for your own good and peace of mind?

#364 Making headway

To make headway, improve your head. ~ B. C. Forbes

- Where have you extended your learning curve?
- What new areas of inquiry could you undertake?
- How might this new learning improve and enrich your life?

#365 Loafing

It is better to have loafed and lost than to have never loafed at all. ~ James Thurber

- Besides 'it's better to have loved and lost...' how much loafing do you do?
- Why is some loafing a good thing?
- How can you resolve for the new year to create a healthy balance between work and play?

****

If you would like a daily Quoteflection, subscribe to my blog at http://365quotequest.blogspot.com

I hope to offer a second volume of 365 Quote Quest in the future. Thank you for your interest.

Paul Cornies